Fear

To my five sons, fearless and beyond reproach!
G. T.

To my children and my godchildren.
V. M.

To all the children I coach in managing their emotions.
S. d. N.

Under the direction of Romain Lizé, CEO, MAGNIFICAT
Editor, MAGNIFICAT: Isabelle Galmiche
Editor, Ignatius: Vivian Dudro
Proofreader: Kathleen Hollenbeck
Graphic Designers: Armelle Riva, Thérèse Jauze
Layout: Gauthier Delauné
Production: Thierry Dubus, Sabine Marioni

Original French edition: *Super peur*
© 2018 by Mame, Paris
© 2021 by MAGNIFICAT, New York • Ignatius Press, San Francisco
ISBN Ignatius Press 978-1-62164-538-2 • ISBN MAGNIFICAT 978-1-949239-67-6

how to HANDLE MY EMOTIONS

Fear

~~~~~~~~~~~~~~~~~~~~~~~

THREE STORIES ABOUT
OVERCOMING FEAR

~~~~~~~~~~~~~~~~~~~~~~~

Gaëlle Tertrais • Violaine Moulière • Ségolène de Noüel

Caroline Modeste

MAGNIFICAT · Ignatius

Contents

Introduction

Fear of the dark, fear of the teacher, fear of jumping off the high dive at the pool... Fear is an emotion you often feel. Sometimes it's more subtle and hidden in your heart: fear of change, fear of rejection, fear of no longer being loved.

In this book, you'll learn the early warning signs of fear: your knees are shaking, your heart is pounding, or your stomach feels tight and sick. Perhaps you freeze, unable to move or speak. You'll also learn how to master your fears and keep them from stopping you from doing what you know is right.

Along with Elliot and Charlotte, you'll discover tools to help you handle this powerful and unpleasant emotion. You'll find out how to respond to fear so that you can act both wisely and bravely.

Remember: God is always with you. When you turn to him in prayer—even a quick "Help me, God!"—he will provide all you need. He will fill you with strength and peace.

1

The New Teacher

This year, Charlotte's teacher is Mrs. Violet. She's awesome! Each morning, she greets the children at the classroom door with a voice as soft as velvet. Charlotte loves that moment. It puts her in a good mood for the whole day.

But this morning, there's no Mrs. Violet. Instead, there's a new teacher in an awful black dress with a mop of straggly hair. As Charlotte enters the classroom, the teacher stares at her with a cold, stern look. Charlotte wishes the earth would swallow her up.

She hurries straight to her desk next to Elliot.

"Have you seen the new teacher?" Charlotte asks him. "Don't you think she looks mean?"

Elliot shrugs his shoulders and says, "Not really. She looks okay to me."

Suddenly, the new teacher walks to her desk and shouts in a piercing voice, "Silence!"

Charlotte gives a start! She feels her tummy tying up in knots, tighter and tighter. Her knees are knocking under her desk. She is trembling. She's almost about to cry!

CHARLOTTE NOTICES
HOW HER BODY
IS REACTING.

All day long, Charlotte has a tummy ache. She cannot eat her favorite potato chips at lunch. She keeps dropping her notebooks and pencils. The moment the teacher glares at her, Charlotte feels as though she's melting into a puddle.

When at last the dismissal bell rings, Charlotte runs off without even waiting for Elliot. Since they live on the same street, they usually walk home together. But today Charlotte walks home alone. "I can tell the new teacher doesn't like me," she thinks. "At one point, she gave me such a beady-eyed look. I'm sure she's nasty. She'll be giving us pop quizzes and tons of homework, and she'll shorten our recess!"

Back home, Charlotte tells her mom all about her terrible day.

"We've got a new teacher. Her name is Mrs. Berg. She's horrible! She shouts! She's nasty! She scares me! I don't want to go back to school!"

CHARLOTTE OWNS
HER EMOTION.

Charlotte blurts all this out in one breath.

Her mom sits down next to her.

"Oh my! She sounds terrible!"

Charlotte nods.

Her mom continues, "You were frightened, and got very upset. When we're scared, we tremble. We go hot and cold, and sometimes our tummy gets tied up in knots. Those are signs to warn us of possible danger. It's important to listen to that feeling. And afterwards, it helps to talk about it."

"Danger? Yes, that's it! This new teacher is really dangerous. I can tell she's really mean. I can see the strange way she looks at me. She doesn't like me!"

"Maybe yes, maybe no! If she yells at you every day for no reason, if she's unfair to you, or if she hurts you, then yes. In that case, you need to protect yourself and talk to a grown-up about it. But, sometimes, the danger isn't as bad as we think. Sometimes it's in our imagination. Maybe Mrs. Berg was just as scared as you about her first day in the classroom. Maybe, to make sure everyone obeyed her, she felt the need to shout. What do you think?"

Charlotte finds it hard to believe that Mrs. Berg might find children scary. But, then again, why not? She thinks it over...

CHARLOTTE
CONSIDERS.

So how do I deal with my fear?

"Tell me," asks Charlotte's mother, "what would you like to see happen to make things better?"

"I just want this teacher to go away! I don't want to be scared anymore!"

CHARLOTTE
RECOGNIZES
HER NEED
FOR SAFETY.

"But you can't just get rid of your schoolteacher!" her mom says. "On the other hand, you *can* do something about your fear of her. Let's see... hmm... What could you do to overcome it? I know! How about if I give you glasses to help you see things differently?"

On a piece of paper, Charlotte's mother draws a funny pair of glasses in the shape of gray clouds and another pair in the shape of bright yellow suns.

"Here you are," she says. "You can choose the way you look at things. If you choose the cloudy glasses, you'll only see your teacher's bad points, and your fear will grow stronger.

"If you choose the sunshiny glasses of kindness, maybe you'll see a teacher who is nervous about her first day in your classroom, but who may have many good sides. Which pair of glasses do you want?"

CHARLOTTE OPTS FOR THE VIRTUE OF KINDNESS.*

Charlotte tries really hard to imagine that her new teacher is just as nice as Mrs. Violet.

Tired of feeling afraid, she chooses the sunshiny glasses!

She agrees to try them, even though deep down, she still feels anxious.

TO OVERCOME HER FEAR, CHARLOTTE USES A TOOL: THE SUNSHINY GLASSES OF KINDNESS.

* A virtue is a habit of choosing to do what is right. For more about virtues see pages 46–47.

15

The next morning, Charlotte again feels that knot in her stomach. She walks to school at a snail's pace. She's in no hurry to get there! When she arrives at the classroom door, there's Mrs. Berg. Yikes!

"Right," thinks Charlotte, "on with the sunshiny glasses!"

Hmm, her teacher looks a tiny bit nicer today. Charlotte gives her a little smile. She walks to her desk but had hardly sat down when Mrs. Berg shouts, "Charlotte! Come to the front of the class to recite your poem!"

"Oh, no!" thinks Charlotte, "She's calling on me first!"

Gone are the sunshiny glasses; gone are the smiles. Charlotte stands up, trembling like a leaf, and moves slowly to the front of the class.

She begins stammering, "The... the... the..."

Neither the owl nor the pussycat nor any other word comes out of her mouth. Her head is spinning. Everything's all jumbled and mixed up.

Then Mrs. Berg comes near her and softly whispers, "The Owl and the Pussy-cat went to sea..."

"What's she doing?" Charlotte wonders. "It seems like she's trying to help me." Charlotte isn't sure, but she pops her sunshiny glasses back on. "Well... why not give Mrs. Berg a chance?" She decides to look at her teacher in a positive light.

CHARLOTTE
PRACTICES
THE VIRTUE
OF KINDNESS.

The teacher leans down to Charlotte and begins very quietly to prompt her again: "The Owl and the Pussy-cat went to sea, in a beautiful pea-green boat."

Through her sunshiny glasses, Charlotte looks at Mrs. Berg with wide eyes. "She's something else, this teacher! There's no one else like her!" she thinks.

Charlotte gives a shy little giggle. Then her teacher giggles, too, and gives her a big smile. Charlotte laughs again, a little louder this time. Then the whole class laughs along with her. Charlotte feels the knot in her stomach untangling. Her head's no longer spinning. She isn't afraid anymore!

Mrs. Berg turns to her with a smile and says, "Shall we take that poem from the top? It will be a snap!"

For the first time, Charlotte looks her straight in the eyes, and begins.

"The Owl and the Pussy-cat went to sea, in a beautiful pea-green boat..."

After she finishes with, "They danced by the light of the moon," Charlotte gives a great sigh of relief. She had managed to recite the whole poem! In her teacher's eyes, she sees a kind twinkle. Best of all, she's managed to overcome her fear! Bravo, Charlotte!

To overcome her fear, Charlotte practiced the virtue of kindness, which helps us to see the good side of people.

2

A Foolish Mistake

It's Saturday! Elliot has invited Charlotte over to play all afternoon. It is a lovely warm day, and they are going to have lots of fun.

When Charlotte arrives, she hears a bird singing.

"Oh, how beautiful!" she says.

"That's Norbert, my little brother's canary," says Elliot. "His godfather brought it back for him from Morocco. He's so proud of it!"

"Oh, please! Can I see it?"

Elliot leads her to the fancy wrought-iron birdcage.

"Ooooh, he's so pretty!" Charlotte says with delight.

Elliot's brother, Archie, never stops reminding everyone to keep the cage carefully shut. Yet Elliot asks Charlotte if she would like to pet the bird. He gently opens the cage door for her to slip in her hand. But before she can touch Norbert, the canary takes off in full flight and escapes through an open window.

Elliot is horrified before the empty cage. What a disaster! His brother will be furious—and heartbroken! He tells Charlotte to go home, but not to breathe a word about what's happened. Then he runs to his room and hides under the bed.

He hopes no one will ever find out what he's done, or he will be in big trouble.

A scream makes him shiver.

"My canary!"

Archie has spotted the empty cage. Elliot hears their father asking Archie what the matter is, then shouting, "Kids, get down here now!"

Elliot breaks out in a cold sweat. He can hear his heart thumping in his chest.

ELLIOT RECOGNIZES
HOW HIS BODY IS
REACTING.

"How can I avoid being found out?" Elliot wonders. He quickly puts on an invisible mask, a smiley face that seems to say, "I didn't do anything; it wasn't me." With his legs wobbling like jelly and his hands trembling, he goes downstairs.

"Norbert's cage wasn't shut properly, and he has escaped. Do you know anything about this?" Dad asks the children, fuming.

Anna, the youngest, shakes her head.

Elliot says nothing, but he starts blushing with shame.

"It was Elliot!" Archie shouts. "I know it was him!"

In a panic, Elliot defends himself. "That's not true! It wasn't me!"

He can feel Dad staring daggers at him. That look weighs so heavy on his heart, Elliot feels as though he's sinking. He wishes he could just disappear.

Then Dad says more calmly, "If the guilty party finds it too hard to tell the truth now, admit it when you're ready."

Elliot quickly runs back to his bedroom. He shuts himself in and tries to slam the door on the fear of what will happen when his father learns the truth. But he hates being a liar! It's just that he's afraid of being punished, of no one loving him anymore because of what he's done.

ELLIOT OWNS HIS
EMOTION.

It's getting dark, but Elliot still hasn't dared to leave his room. And now, Mom is calling from the stairway, "Dinner's ready!"

Elliot really doesn't want to eat dinner with his family. He is trembling again and feeling weak in the knees! "How can I face my family like this?" he wonders. He puts his phony smile back on and goes downstairs.

At the table, Elliot is sure everyone is looking at him. Archie starts crying again.

"You know," Dad said, "when I was eight years old, I remember hiding to avoid telling your grandma that I'd broken the clock case when I was playing Tarzan."

"Really?" exclaimed Archie between sobs.

"Afraid so, and I was scared stiff. I kept it secret, but with a heavy heart. I felt so alone! In the end, I had to make a choice: either I could keep what I'd done to myself and avoid punishment, or I could find the courage to tell the truth. Telling the truth would be the harder thing to do, but it would lift a great weight from my shoulders!"

"And then what happened? What did you choose?"

"The truth! I plucked up my courage and admitted what I'd done. Grandma was very angry, of course, but she didn't tell me off as badly as I thought she would. On the other hand, I had to help your granddad fix the clock case—and that wasn't easy, I can tell you!"

As they clear the table, Dad stops with a stack of dishes and casually adds, "You know, the person who let out the canary can just whisper the truth quietly in someone's ear or write it down on a slip of paper."

Back in his room, Elliot recalls everything his dad has said.

He thinks it over...

ELLIOT CONSIDERS.

So how do I deal with my fear?

He can't stand keeping up this lie anymore! He wants to be free of it!

ELLIOT RECOGNIZES HIS NEED FOR THE TRUTH.

He takes a deep breath, and, like Zorro, he rips off his invisible mask.

TO FREE HIMSELF OF HIS FEAR, ELLIOT USES A TOOL: HE REMOVES HIS MASK.

He makes up his mind: he's going to tell the truth.

ELLIOT OPTS FOR THE VIRTUE OF HONESTY.

On a piece of paper, he writes:

Sorry, Archie, about Norbert. I didn't do it on purpose. I just wanted to show him to Charlotte. I'm really sorry.
Elliot

He did it! Elliot feels a little relief. He crumples the paper up in a ball and aims it through Archie's half-open door. Plaf! Bullseye!

He rushes back to hide in his room and waits with a pounding heart. The reply isn't long in coming: Archie shoots into his room like a cannonball, furious and ready to punch him!

"It was you! I knew it! I hate you!"

Elliot says he's sorry, begging Archie to understand that it was a mistake. But Archie doesn't care. He isn't even interested when Elliot offers him his favorite marble. It's not that easy, telling the truth!

Suddenly, at the window, Elliot spots Norbert perched on the top branch of a cherry tree. Maybe he can make up for what he's done! He whispers a few words in Archie's ear, and at last, Archie's face lights up! They both run to their dad's workshop. They know he'll be happy to help them.

It takes them a while, but they manage it: they build a nice little birdhouse for Archie's canary and hang it on the cherry tree. And guess what? Norbert decides to nest in it! Archie jumps for joy, and Elliot smiles. The truth has set Elliot and Norbert free, and his fear has flown the coop.

To overcome his fear, Elliot practices the virtue of honesty, which means being truthful in our words and our deeds.

Help!
The Water's Rising!

Charlotte and Elliot are spending the weekend at the seashore. Their families are staying together at the home of Charlotte's aunt Agatha and her cousin Clementine.

On Saturday, Aunt Agatha takes the children to the beach while the grown-ups go for a long walk. Wow, a whole day of playing, fishing, and swimming—what joy!

"The last one in is a rotten egg!" shouts Elliot as he sprints toward the water.

Charlotte and the other children are hard on his heels as they run across the beach and jump into the waves with whoops of laughter.

Then, Felix, Charlotte's big brother, has a great idea.

"Hey! Look over there," he calls out, pointing to a strip of large rocks in the distance. "I bet we can catch crabs! C'mon."

Elliot, Archie, Clementine, and Charlotte follow him down the beach to where they can no longer see Aunt Agatha tanning herself on the sand.

Felix turns toward the water and starts walking toward the rocks, saying, "There are plenty of crabs over there—you'll see!"

But seeing that the tide is coming in, Charlotte feels uneasy and stops in her tracks.

"What's up, Charlotte? Aren't you coming?" Elliot asks.

"Ummm, I'm not sure. The tide is coming in. Isn't it dangerous? Look at the sign over there. It says: 'No swimming. Dangerous riptides.'"

Elliot breaks out in laughter and says, "There's no danger! It's low tide. We still have time."

But Charlotte can see that the water has already risen higher than a moment ago. She feels her stomach knotting up. She can't take another step forward. Trembling a bit, she stays where she is.

CHARLOTTE RECOGNIZES HOW HER BODY IS REACTING.

"Oh, you scaredy-cat! Crybaby!" Felix teases her, looking back over his shoulder.

"That's not true!" she shouts, trying not to cry.

But in her head, a little voice is whispering to her, "What a dope I am. I'm too frightened to follow them. He's right, I'm just a scaredy-cat! Come on, let's go!"

CHARLOTTE OWNS HER EMOTION.

But it's true: Charlotte is afraid.

She knows very well that, if she follows them, she risks drowning. But, if she doesn't, they'll all make fun of her. And she can't stand that. So, she thinks for a moment.

CHARLOTTE CONSIDERS.

So, how do I deal with my fear?

Does she go? Or does she not go? Charlotte can't decide. She tries to think of what could help her. What would Mom or Aunt Agatha say?

CHARLOTTE RECOGNIZES HER NEED FOR GOOD ADVICE.

"That's it! I've got it!" she thinks, remembering when Aunt Agatha had told her how fast the tide comes in at this spot. And Charlotte trusts her. She plucks up her courage, clenches her fists, and feels strength rising up within her.

TO RELIEVE HER FEAR, CHARLOTTE USES A TOOL: CLENCHING HER FISTS.

"That does it, I'm not going!" she says to herself.

CHARLOTTE OPTS FOR THE VIRTUE OF STRENGTH.

She shouts to the others, who are already on the first rocks of the little outcropping, "You're crazy! Come back! The tide's rising. You'll get stranded!"

CHARLOTTE PRACTICES THE VIRTUE OF STRENGTH.

But they don't want to listen. Felix shouts to her, "We're not scaredy-cats, like you!"

And they all start laughing at her, even Elliot, her friend.

She is hurt but decides to stay put, hoping that the parents will soon return from their walk. In the meantime, she gathers seashells.

There are spiral ones, pink scallops, cockles, and tiny bright and shiny white shells. There are so many that Charlotte forgets about everything else.

Suddenly, she hears shouts. She looks to the rocks and sees that her companions are surrounded by water and waving at her. They are stranded! But where's Archie? Oh no! He has

fallen into the water and can't climb out! He's going to drown!

Charlotte's heart races. A lump in her throat is so huge she can hardly breathe. Once again, Charlotte is frightened, really frightened! She freezes in a panic. Where can she get help?

"Aunt Agatha!" she immediately thinks. She clenches her fists really tight to give herself courage and runs off across the beach toward her aunt.

CHARLOTTE PRACTICES THE VIRTUE OF STRENGTH.

With each step, her feet seem to sink into the sand or get scraped by rocks. Oww! She runs faster than a bullet. It's incredible; she feels as though she's flying! Her fear has put wings on her heels!

At last, she reaches Aunt Agatha. All out of breath, she tells her what's happened: the rocks, the crabs, the sign, the tide, and Archie, who is about to drown!

Aunt Agatha doesn't lose a second. She runs straight to the rescue station to find a lifeguard.

He grabs a red buoy and runs toward the out-cropping. He jumps into the water and swims with all his might against the tide. Within seconds, he's by Archie's side. He pulls Archie onto the buoy just as the young boy is about to give up and stop treading water.

Then, two more lifeguards arrive in a motor-boat to pick up the other stranded children. Soon, everyone is back on shore, safe and sound.

Aunt Agatha is pretty angry, but the children look so upset and sorry that she just frowns and takes Archie in her arms to warm him up.

"And there weren't even any crabs," grumbles Felix to hide his embarrassment.

The lifeguard seizes the moment to teach him a lesson: "You should never have gone out there; didn't you see the sign? Swimming is forbidden there! If it weren't for this brave little girl, I don't like to think what might have happened to you!"

"Oh, that... It's only because she was afraid," Felix smugly replies.

"Exactly! And her fear is what saved you. It's important to listen to our fears. They warn us of danger."

"I was a little bit scared too, but I was ashamed to say so," Archie adds in a timid little voice. "The others would have made fun of me."

"Being frightened is nothing to be ashamed of!" the lifeguard continues. "The next time you feel like that, take time to listen to your fears. They can keep you out of a lot of trouble!"

Then Archie turns to Charlotte and says, "Thank you, Charlotte. Thank goodness you were there!"

Suddenly, Elliot claps his hands and shouts, "Three cheers for Charlotte! The bravest girl ever!"

The lifeguard nods and says, "He's right! You're the heroine of the hour! It's thanks to you this boy was saved!"

Then, removing his lifeguard medal, he places it around her neck and declares, "That's for you. You truly deserve it!"

Back at the house, despite her scraped feet, Charlotte is so filled with joy that she feels she'll explode! And now she knows a secret: when she needs to be strong, she'll remember to clench her fists. Then ta-da! Somehow, she'll find the courage!

To overcome her fear, Charlotte practices the virtue of strength to give her the courage to confront a difficult situation.

WHAT HAVE YOU LEARNED FROM THESE STORIES?

Fear isn't a pleasant emotion. But it can be useful to warn us of danger.

HAVE YOU EVER NOTICED HOW YOU FEEL WHEN YOU'RE AFRAID?

Maybe your heart starts racing or you have a sudden tummy ache. Perhaps you tremble, feel a lump in your throat, or get goosebumps. You might even have trouble breathing.

Perhaps something seems so hard or scary that you say to yourself: "I can't do it", "I won't manage it", or "I don't want to do this."

Draw here how your body reacts when you're afraid.

THE EMOTION METER

According to the type of event and our own personality, our fear can be greater or smaller.

We may start out feeling CONCERNED, and then grow WORRIED, or ANXIOUS. The next thing we know, we are STRESSED and, finally, PANICKED!

How about you? Can you measure your fear?

FEAR IS USEFUL!

• Fear protects us from a real or imagined danger. For example, when Charlotte fears her teacher is nasty, it's an imagined danger. But when she fears drowning, the danger is real.

• Fear spurs us on to outdo ourselves: then it becomes a super-charged source of energy. For example, the fear of seeing Archie drown causes Charlotte to fly to his rescue.

VIRTUES COME TO THE AID OF OUR EMOTIONS!

In each story, Elliot and Charlotte choose a virtue to overcome their fear.

Do you know what a virtue is? **A virtue is a habit of choosing to do what is right.** At first, that takes effort. But with time, it becomes easier and easier. It's a little like learning to ride a bike!

SPOTLIGHT ON THE VIRTUE OF STRENGTH

You know what it means to be strong. It's having the muscles to lift a heavy weight or to run really fast.

The virtue of strength is a little like that. It's **the ability of the soul to be strong and brave in order to do what's right.** The more you train yourself in its practice, the more you'll be able to confront difficulties and move on!

Strength, often called **fortitude**, is one of **the four cardinal virtues**, along with temperance, prudence, and justice.

Why **cardinal**? Like the four cardinal points on a compass: north, south, east, and west, the cardinal virtues point you in the right direction to lead your life safely and with joy and confidence!

It's not always easy to practice the virtues, so Elliot and Charlotte both used tools to help them! Find those tools in each story and link them to their virtues.

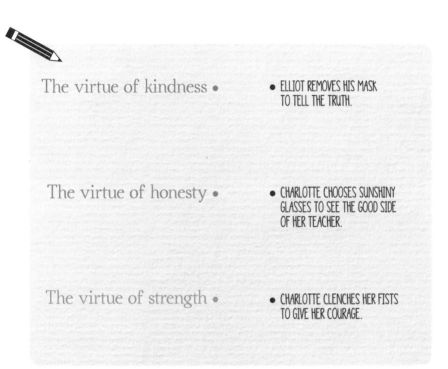

The virtue of kindness •

• ELLIOT REMOVES HIS MASK TO TELL THE TRUTH.

The virtue of honesty •

• CHARLOTTE CHOOSES SUNSHINY GLASSES TO SEE THE GOOD SIDE OF HER TEACHER.

The virtue of strength •

• CHARLOTTE CLENCHES HER FISTS TO GIVE HER COURAGE.

now
it's your turn
to put the virtues
into practice!

THE PATHWAY THROUGH EMOTIONS

An emotion is a reaction to an event perceived by our five senses. It tells us we need something. Then it's up to us to work through it! To better understand what's happening, follow Elliot and Charlotte along the pathway of emotions!

I OWN MY EMOTION.

I ACT

So now, how do I deal with my emotion? Let's break it down into steps.

1. EXPERIENCING A STIMULUS

I hear someone's words or sense an unpleasant attitude. (Perhaps they make threats, shout, or call me names.)
I experience an event (such as an accident, a setback, or a challenging situation like a dark room or deep water).

2. SENSING MY EMOTIONAL REACTION

I sense: my heart racing, my stomach in knots, my legs trembling, and so on.
I feel: helpless, paralyzed, unable to think or act.

3. IDENTIFYING THE EMOTION

I ask myself: What's happening to me?
I realize: I feel scared.

4. OWNING THE EMOTION

I own the emotion for what it is: neither good nor bad.

HOW WILL I H MY EMOTIO

MAKING A DECISION

oose an attitude to take:
ll look for the good in others, tell the
th, or be strong to do what's right.

TAKING ACTION
se the tools that will help me progress:
ting on sunny glasses, taking off the
sk of lies, or clenching my fists to
engthen my resolve.

PRACTICING DAY AFTER DAY

HAPPINESS

Love, peace, joy,
respect, self-worth,
and so on.

10

9

TEMPTATION

REGRET

8

UNHAPPINESS

Thinking the worst,
telling lies, being unable
to rise to the
occasion.

I STOP TO THINK...

5

*How will I handle
my emotion?*

5. DISCERNING WHAT TO DO
I think about what's really good for me and others.

6. RECOGNIZING MY NEED
I identify what prompted my fear.
Perhaps I need to be reassured that I am safe
or encouraged to be honest and bold.

7. LOOKING FOR A MEANS TO RESPOND
TO MY NEED
Virtues: Kindness, honesty, strength.
Vices: Meanness, dishonesty, cowardice.

VICE
OR
VIRTUE ?

From their earliest years, children are able to identify specific emotions, and from the age of reason, they have the capacity to deal with them. This unique series on the emotions responds to that potential with both faith and guidance, offering a virtuous pathway to a happy life.

As a parent, teacher, or educator, how do you react to a child's fear? Do you tell him that it's nothing, and that he shouldn't worry? Or do you agree that something is causing fear?

The tried-and-true approaches in this book can help you find a healthy way to help a child handle emotions.

What is fear?

Fear is an unpleasant—sometimes very unpleasant—emotion. It can rise up suddenly or creep in little by little. Sometimes our reaction is to ignore it or to be ashamed of it.

How to express one's fear?

Fear takes many different forms: tummy upsets, trembling, a racing heart. The whole body is set off when we're confronted by a possible danger.

A burst of adrenaline allows the body to find the energy needed to react, whether that be fight or flight.

In our stories, the fear of seeing Archie drown gives Charlotte the strength to run for help. Elliot has done a foolish thing and is afraid no one will love him anymore; he hides to protect himself from punishment he knows is coming. In the classroom, Charlotte wants to protect herself from her teacher by refusing to go back to school.

How can you help a child through fear?

TO START WITH, AVOID EXPRESSING ANY JUDGMENT OF FEAR. EVEN IF YOU FIND IT RIDICULOUS, TAKE THE CHILD'S EMOTION SERIOUSLY.

• **Choose the right moment.**
And as soon as possible! Over time, fears can build up and block a child's development. Avoid that pitfall by addressing the subject quickly.

• **Be there for the child.**
Show you are giving the child your full attention. Put your cellphone and your chores to one side and concentrate on the child. Look at your child or not, according to the situation. (Children can feel ashamed of being afraid, and looking them in the eye may make them feel uneasy.)

Your *calm* presence will provide a reassuring atmosphere for the child.

• **Listen.**
Invite the child to tell you what he is feeling and to name the emotion. You could suggest that the child evaluate the fear on a scale of 1 to 10 to help you better pinpoint the extent of the emotion.

To allow children to express their emotions, it's important to give them time to find their words and finish their sentences.

THEN, HELP THE CHILD TO REFLECT.

Recognize the need.

Help the child to identify his needs. Perhaps it's to be reassured or protected, to be respected when feeling under attack, or to deal with an unknown situation such as a move to a new school, the birth of a sibling, the illness of a loved one, and so on.

Be careful! If we don't deal with our fear, the emotion can get stronger and stronger each time we're confronted by the same kind of situation. The physical discomfort can grow and get worse.

If you don't manage to calm a fear that's blocking the child—or blocking you—don't hesitate to consult a professional. A deep emotional wound may be at the bottom of that fear.

Accept responsibility.

You are the child's guide, but you can't act in his place. Give advice that helps the child to decide what to do to handle fear:

"What about if you...?"

"How might you...?"

"What would happen if you...?"

Make sure the child is conscious of his own responsibility for the decision, and support it.

Fear and lies.

Young children rarely intend or are aware of doing harm when they lie; they're afraid of disappointing others, of being punished, or of being shamed. What's real and what's imaginary is still very muddled in their minds.

It's the role of adults, and of parents in particular, to form a child's conscience by gently but firmly bringing him back to reality.

What do you do when a child tells a lie?

As the adult, don't show your disappointment or your exasperation. That kind of attitude makes it more difficult for a child to admit to a lie. The problem of dishonesty lies with the child, so it's up to him to own up to it, even if you've seen through the lie.

In discussing it with the child, take time to consider what you say, and be careful not to equate the act with the person. Don't call him a liar; that will only imprison the child in this vice.

To help a child admit a lie, don't make accusations either (e.g., "You're talking nonsense" or "You're lying"). Instead, go over the facts ("The birdcage was opened, then badly shut, and the bird escaped. Who opened the cage and forgot to close it properly?").

Once the facts have been accepted, you can, with the child, judge whether it's a case of a thoughtless mistake or a willful bad action. Then thank the child for having told the truth and reassure the child that you still love him even though you do not like what he did. That will encourage the child to tell the truth in the future.

Finally, consider with the child how to repair the harm that's been done: to ask for forgiveness, to do something to make up for it, to replace what's been broken with his own money. In the case of willful wrongdoing, the child can be encouraged to go to confession.

THE PATHWAY OF VICE

This collection encourages children to rely on the virtues to transform their emotions into positive energy.

Vice is the opposite of virtue. Like every other vice, repeated lying takes hold and becomes like a default setting. The conscience becomes blunted and, after a time, convinces us that our version of events is true. Once it's set in, vice bears bitter fruits: stealing, deceit, betrayal, unfaithfulness, the mistrust of those around us, and isolation, among others. This vice can be fought with the virtue of honesty!

And remember: the virtuous pathway leads to openness with others and to true happiness!

Printed in June 2021, by Dimograf, Poland.

Job number 21027

Printed in compliance with the Consumer Protection Safety Act, 2008.